A LOOK AT TRANSFER

In A Nutshell

series

A LOOK AT TRANSFER

Seven Strategies That Work

In A Nutshell
collection

Robin J. Fogarty • Brian M. Pete

CORWIN
A SAGE Company

For information:

Corwin
A SAGE Company
2455 Teller Road
Thousand Oaks,
    California 91320
(800) 233-9936
Fax: (800) 417-2466
www.corwinpress.com

SAGE Ltd.
1 Oliver's Yard
55 City Road
London EC1Y 1SP
United Kingdom

SAGE India Pvt. Ltd.
B 1/I 1 Mohan Cooperative
    Industrial Area
Mathura Road,
    New Delhi 110 044
India

SAGE Asia-Pacific Pte. Ltd.
33 Pekin Street #02-01
Far East Square
Singapore 048763

Printed in the United States of America

A catalog record of this book is available from the Library of Congress.

ISBN: 978-0-9717-3326-8

This book is printed on acid-free paper.

09   10   11   12   13   10   9   8   7   6   5   4   3   2   1

Contents

■ □ ■ □ ■

■□■□■

Preface

The Question That Started It All

Many years ago, several participants stopped to talk to me after a workshop on critical and creative thinking. As the first woman stepped up to me, she reached out to shake my hand and greeted me with these words, "This was great! I really enjoyed the day, but I can't use these ideas with my kids or my content." Needless to say, I was not only disappointed in the remark but also bothered by my inadequacy to reach the participant in a relevant way.

As I turned to leave, another woman plunged toward me and hugged me with all her might. She gushed with compliments about the day and said something I remember vividly to this day, "You have changed my teaching forever. I can never go back to what I was doing before today. Now, I know too much about how to make my kids think. Thank you for making it so easy for me to take these ideas back to my classroom," and off she went with a bounce in her step and a huge smile on her face.

The contrast between the two participants was so striking it took me a minute to recover. I remember thinking to myself, "What is it I did for the second woman that I did *not* do for the first woman. Why can one see *no* relevant possibilities, while the other one sees myriad ways to use the material we worked with today? What might I do differently to foster transfer for all the participants?" That was the question that plagued me for quite some time following that day.

At one point, as I tried to describe to a colleague the incident of the woman who did not see relevant connections from the workshop to her classroom behavior, the image of an ostrich with his head in the sand came to mind. The metaphor suggested that, in this case, the learner had her "head in the sand" (intentionally or not) and was missing the obvious connections that others had seen. Somehow, the message was not connecting.

This metaphor was to become a lasting image that guided my work in professional development. This image haunted me during my early doctoral studies. Ultimately, it was this image that shaped my dissertation thesis. Six "bird" metaphors that describe levels of transfer are derived from my eighteen years as a consultant/staff developer in education and my dissertation.

Over time, as my partner and colleague, Brian Pete, and I have worked with this idea, seven transfer strategies have emerged and become clearer and more purposeful in our work with teachers. These seven strategies have proven to be powerful and empowering for teacher participants as they bridge the learning from the staff room to the classroom.

Enjoy.

Robin J. Fogarty

Chicago, 2003

■□■□■

Acknowledgments

Our thanks and gratitude to all the educational researchers/writers who have tackled this idea of transfer. Among those notables are: Madeline Hunter, David Perkins, Gabriele Solomon, Robert Swartz, Bruce Joyce, and Beverly Showers. Their work illuminates our work enormously. Our thanks and gratitude to our production crew, both on in North America and abroad. Without the supreme efforts of these dedicated people in editing, designing, printing, and shipping, we would not have this book to share with teachers.

Dedication

To
Coleman Whitaker Vickary,
who has transferred many hobbies into enterprising businesses.

Transfer in Theory: Six Levels

The theory of creative transfer involves two distinguishable clusters of transfer: simple or near transfer and complex or remote transfer. *Simple* transfer is almost automatic because it "hugs " the original learning situation and takes little effort to apply the skill or idea to a novel situation. *Complex* transfer requires thought and effort because it is transfer that is remote from the original learning and takes conscious awareness to find connections or to "bridge" ideas to novel situations that make relevant transfer.

> **The theory of creative transfer involves two distinguishable clusters of transfer.**

Within the realm of simple transfer, there seem to be three levels of transfer: (a) missing the opportunity to transfer, (b) duplicating and practicing exactly as learned, and (c) replicating the learning by tailoring it slightly. Within the realm of complex transfer, there also are three levels of application that seem to occur: (d) integrating by assimilating the new into the old, (e) propagating or spreading the strategies through intentional mapping, and (f) innovating with creative flair. Together these six distinct levels of transfer comprise the continuum from no apparent transfer to purposeful, relevant and observable transfer.

These situational dispositions toward transfer are given metaphorical bird names that frame the various levels of transfer in highly descriptive ways and provide an easy way for adult learners to talk about transfer with their peers (Figure 1.1).

■□■□■

Levels of Transfer

Bird Metaphor	Transfer Theory	Learning Theory
SIMPLE		
Ollie, Head-in-the-Sand Ostrich	Misses	Overlooks
Dan, Drilling Woodpecker	Practices	Duplicates
Laura, Look-alike Penguin	Hugs	Replicates
COMPLEX		
Jonathan Livingston, Seagull	Personalizes	Integrates
Cathy, Carrier Pigeon	Bridges	Propagates
Samantha, Soaring Eagle	Invents	Innovates

Figure 1.1

In the discussions that follow for each level within the two clusters of transfer, each level is identified with its bird of transfer, described with its prime transfer characteristic, illustrated with an example of learning tennis skills, and depicted in a figure that displays what the level of transfer looks and sounds like for teachers as adult learners.

The purpose of the figures is to further understanding of how to recognize the various levels of transfer. The more aware learners are of the apparent levels of transfer, the more they are able to foster relevant application and use of the concepts and skills being learned. In addition, the figures not only provide a look at specific behaviors that signal the learning for the staff developer, but they also inform the adult learner for self-monitoring and self-assessment. Readers may easily add examples to these sets as they become more familiar with the concept of transfer.

The more aware learners are of the apparent levels of transfer, the more they are able to foster relevant application and use of the concepts and skills being learned.

Please note: For a similar look at transfer in the classroom with student learners, see the appendix. The six levels are depicted there, with appropriate classroom examples.

Simple Transfer

The simple transfer cluster involves those three levels of transfer that miss, duplicate, or replicate the training situation. Again, this transfer is easy, and almost automatic.

■□■□■

Overlooks: Ollie, the Head-in-the-Sand Ostrich

Representing the absence of transfer of any kind, Ollie depicts the learner who overlooks opportunities for transfer. This learner seems unaware of the relevance of and overlooks applications that may seem obvious to others. Ollie misses the point of the strategy or skill, as though the "shot didn't take." For example, after a tennis lesson that focused on how to grip the racket, the learner that is at the Ollie level of transfer ignores the newly presented procedure and persists in gripping the racket in the old way.

There is also the Ollie who intentionally overlooks or misses opportunities to use the new ideas. This learner transfer is characterized by the notion that the application is not worthy of doing. Most people have been Ollies at some point in their learning experiences, so this is not a judgmental model. It is a model of transfer with the goal of making learners more aware of their learning behavior.

Figure 1.2 shows what this first level of transfer looks and sounds like following a staff development session. These behaviors signal the leader to foster transfer and relevance in some way.

■ □ ■ □ ■

The Adult Learner: A Look at Ollie, the Head-in-the-Sand Ostrich

Looks Like...	Sounds Like...
The teacher who, usually unintentionally, overlooks the opportunity to use the new learning is an Ollie. She persists in the old or former way because she misses the point; she just doesn't see the relevance and doesn't make the critical connection to her work setting. However, sometimes, Ollie sees the point, but intentionally chooses not to use the idea because she thinks it's inappropriate or not a good fit.	*"Great Session, but it won't work with my kids or my content."* *"I'll never use this because the curriculum is already too crowded. There's no time for this stuff."* *"This was fun, but not relevant to my needs."* *"Yeah, but..."*

Figure 1.2

Duplicates: Dan, the Drilling Woodpecker

Dan signifies the learner who drills and practices learning exactly as it was presented. The transfer becomes drill, drill, drill. This level of transfer is at an almost automatic stage. The learner does not move beyond copying the pattern. For example, the tennis player learns the steps and the swing for the backhand and practices the move faithfully until it is grooved. There is no attempt to personalize or customize the learning to fit the learner's needs better. Yet, this is a stab at transfer and application, to be celebrated.

Figure 1.3 illustrates the look and sound for this level of transfer. Again, it is a cue for the leader about where the learner is in terms of applications and uses of the newly learned skill.

The Adult Learner: A Look at Dan, the Drilling Woodpecker

Looks Like...	Sounds Like...
This is the teacher who takes the idea to the classroom, practicing it exactly as it is presented in the workshop, with no fluctuations. This is a Dan. He continues to drill, drill, drill, like the woodpecker, duplicating the effort, precisely, each time. In this level of transfer, the teacher uses the idea as a single, focused activity, rather than as a generic strategy that can be tailored according to various application needs. Yet, this learner is transferring the new idea in a simple transfer model, so the goal of application and use is realized.	*"May I have a copy of your transparency. I want to use that with my kids."* *"Where can I get the resource on the brain and memory that you used? I want to do exactly what we just did with my class."* *"This is a perfect graphic organizer for my next class. I didn't write on the handout page so I could use it right away."*

Figure 1.3

Replicates: Laura, the Look-Alike Penguin

Laura is the learner who applies new learning in narrow ways, restricting the applications to one kind or one way, so the applications tend to all look alike. However, transfer at this level, although still simple or near transfer, does show indications of personalization. The learner tailors the idea in

■□■□■

such a way that it works perfectly for her circumstances. This change or adjustment might be minor, but it is significant as it distinguishes this level from Dan, the Drilling Woodpecker at the duplicator level. Lauras adapt the new ideas in personally relevant ways. For example, a tennis player personalizes how he tosses the ball for the serve by using a particular pre-toss procedure that eventually becomes his trademark serving style.

Figure 1.4 shows one view of the replicator level of transfer.

The Adult Learner: A Look at Laura, the Look-Alike Penguin

Looks Like...	Sounds Like...
Another simple transfer, but with some slight changes to make it fit, is shown by the teacher who tailors or customizes the idea for her kids or her content. But, after that shift is made, the applications all look alike. She does not vary from the pattern she establishes; all the applications look quite similar. She differentiates slightly, but truly "hugs" the original learning and executes a nearly automatic application, a near transfer, close to the original.	*"I use the web graphic to do character analysis each time we are working with fictional pieces."* *"I used your log lead-in statements, but translated them into French for my first year kids."* *" To do this experiment with my kids, I need to adjust the problems to fit elementary school age kids."*

Figure 1.4

Complex Transfer

The complex cluster of transfer levels involves those levels of transfer that integrate, propagate, or innovate based on the training situation. Complex transfer requires mindfulness. It needs to be bridged!

Integrates: Jonathon Livingston Seagull

Jonathan Livingston Seagull depicts the learner who subtly integrates the new learning smoothly with former ways. The transfer is implicit rather than explicit and Jonathan often says, "I already do this." This learner seems to have a raised consciousness or acute awareness of the learning, but is never really overt about the transfer. Following the tennis example, this learner takes the strategy of "playing the net" and seems to integrate the move directly into the tennis game without explicit practice at the net. It is a smooth, almost seamless, application, yet, perhaps, used more frequently than before because of a raised consciousness about its effectiveness.

Figure 1.5 illustrates the transfer level of integrating.

■□■□■

The Adult Learner: A Look at Jonathan Livingston Seagull

Looks Like...	Sounds Like...
"There is nothing new in education." Illustrated by this level of transfer, an idea that is somewhat familiar to the teacher is now integrated subtly into an existing repertoire. The key here is that the strategy is performed with a raised consciousness. The application is executed with more explicit awareness and deliberate refinements. In this level of complex transfer, the new learning is not really all that new. It smacks of earlier ideas and the learner makes direct connections to that former mental model. In this case the new learning is absorbed into earlier patterns.	"I already do these kinds of open-ended problems, but now I'm more deliberate in my approach and I find myself consciously choosing to use the strategy." "I haven't really used case studies explicitly, because I already do something very similar." "I'm so aware of these reflection strategies, now. I had forgotten how effective they are." "It's so nice to re-discover an old friend…using higher order questions was always a great strategy. Now, I am revisiting them with renewed vigor."

Figure 1.5

Propagates: Cathy, the Carrier Pigeon

Cathy carries the ideas to lots of new places, quite intentionally. She maps the idea and "propagates" by creating many new applications in many new situations. Cathy is a natural learner, eager to find a use for what she is learning. She is pragmatic and deliberate in her applications. She often sees applications before the learning is complete as she thinks ahead to how she might use some idea. The tennis example might be that she learns about terry headbands and wristbands to absorb the sweat during play, and she immediately uses a headband in her aerobics class. The next day, she uses a headband in her spinning class and a week later, she uses a headband on her 5k "Run for the Zoo." These are deliberate applications, creatively propagated through many different activities because Cathy has generalized the idea from the specific situation to other similar situations.

Figure 1.6 shows the look like and sound like examples for the transfer level of propagating.

The Adult Learner: A Look at Cathy, the Carrier Pigeon

Looks Like...	Sounds Like...
This level of transfer epitomizes the "star" participant who tries everything very deliberately. Cathy consciously transfers ideas to various content, strategizing and mapping the ideas intentionally. This is the teacher who generalizes new applications easily. She associates ideas and bridges them into purposeful applications. This learner naturally sees tons of connections that are relevant and useful. Cathy is the ideal learner in training, because she innately understands that she is there to get ideas and to take them back to her classroom.	*"I have three ways already in my mind about how I can use the fishbone graphic."* *"This matrix is perfect for my project next week, and I even think it might work with the lesson I'm doing today."* *"I love carrying this idea about service learning from one application to the next. It's so easy to bridge it to different contexts."* *"I can't wait to try these data questions with my kids and my family, too."*

Figure 1.6

■□■□■

Innovates: Samantha, the Soaring Eagle

Samantha illustrates the highest level and most complex kind of transfer. This learner leaps to transfer and beyond. He creates, invents, innovates, and enhances every idea with such elaboration, finesse, and grace that the original application is sometimes blurred. The transfer seems unique and is a metamorphosis of sorts. To look at an example with a tennis player, this learner takes the concept of a strategic play and outperforms her opponent with elaborate changes in pacing, positioning, and demeanor. The shifts in play become part of this player's repertoire and, over time, become part of the legend of this player's fame.

Figure 1.7 looks at the behaviors of the final level of transfer, innovating.

■ □ ■ □ ■

An Adult Learner: A Look at Samantha, the Soaring Eagle

Looks Like...	Sounds Like...
Sam "flies" with an idea. This learner truly innovates and creates unique applications from the original ideas. "High flyers" often go way beyond the first idea and invent one of their own, enhancing the original tremendously. This learner is a risk-taker, has high energy, exhibits fluency and flexibility with ideas, and often elaborates on an idea with grace and skill. This is the learner who thinks out of the box, naturally, and often produces ideas that are outrageous, yet purposeful and clever.	*"You have changed my teaching forever. This session on using data to make instructional decisions was the key I needed."* *" I can never go back to the old way, now I know too much about how to help kids read in content areas."* *"I've been thinking about this all weekend and I have a "genius" idea about how to use this information on nutrition and the brain."* *"This has been the greatest workshop for me. I feel like I have a fresh window on my teaching. I will be setting high expectations for my kids"*

Figure 1.7

Transfer in Action: Seven Strategies

Rationale

Educators will know that professional development works when they pay as much attention to the transfer strategies as they pay to the initiative itself. They will know that professional development works when they deliberately and intentionally promote and foster transfer as part and parcel of everything they do to support instruction. They will know that professional development works when they see evidence of the strategies incorporated into classroom lessons, when they see expanded teaching repertoires, and when they see authentic evidence of increased student achievement.

Strategies

Seven research-based strategies (Fogarty, 1989) help focus teacher training on explicit and relevant transfer of ideas into the classroom and help achieve that goal of robust teaching repertoires for every teacher. These strategies are tried-and-true, teacher-tested techniques. They bridge professional development content from the staff training setting directly into k-12 classroom settings. These seven strategies (Figure 2.1) are:

1. Understanding Transfer

2. Setting Expectations for Transfer

3. Modeling With Authentic Artifacts

4. Reflecting on the Levels of Transfer

5. Plotting an Application

6. Trying Something Immediately

7. Dialoguing with Hugging/Bridging Lead-ins.

The discussions of each strategy focus on examples of fostering transfer for teachers as adult learners.

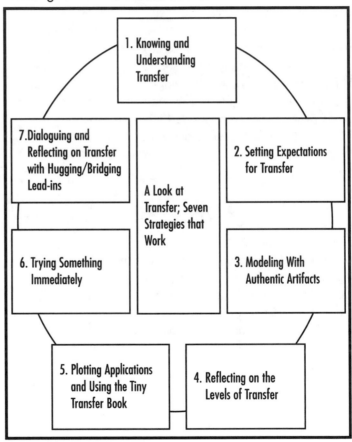

Figure 2.1

Understanding Transfer

Know about and understand the concept of transfer.
Teachers need to read about the findings about transfer and
reflect on their relevance to the teaching and
learning process in the classroom and in the
staff room. All teaching is for transfer; all
learning is for transfer. To extend learning, to
bridge the old and the new, and to lead
learners toward relevant transfer and use
across academic content is the mission of
sound classroom practice and professional development
experiences.

> **All teaching is for transfer; all learning is for transfer.**

In some cases, the transfer of learning is obvious or
simple (Fogarty, 1989) because the learned skills seem close
to the skill situation to which they are transferred. In adult
learners, when teachers are learning about cooperative
learning by participating in cooperative groups during the
training, the learning situation "hugs"(Perkins & Salomon,
1988) the classroom situation. It is easy to use the same
strategies in the classroom with students because the transfer
is clear. The teacher has experienced the strategy and has
been immersed in it, so transfer is a natural outcome.

However, in other instances, learning for adults in a
training situation seems far removed or remote from transfer
in the classroom. When teachers are learning
about infusing sophisticated thinking skills, such
as inferring, into their lessons, transfer is more
remote and bridging the skill into various
content is harder (Perkins & Salomon, 1988).
Although the skill of inferring is demonstrated
and practiced in a language arts example
during training, the chemistry teacher, the

> **Learning for adults in a training situation seems far removed or remote from transfer in the classroom.**

physical education teacher, and the American history teacher see making inferences quite differently. For the chemistry teacher, inferring is learning the difference between an observation and a conjecture concerning a science experiment. For the gym teacher, inferring is about students theorizing about their fitness from data collected and graphed throughout the term. For the history teacher, inferring is when students drawing conclusions as they relate historical ideas to current events of the day. When it is hard to understand how the skill applies directly in another content, transfer is remote and obscure—*complex* (Fogarty, 1989). In these situations, bridging strategies are used to foster relevant transfer.

Setting Expectations

Set expectations for transfer of learning. Setting expectations for transfer harnesses the same power that comes into play when one is setting goals (Haycock, 1998; Schmoker, 1998). Think about it. When an administrative assistant attends a day of software training, the expectation is that she will use the software immediately in her work setting. In adult learning situations, teachers traditionally have had no mandate for expecting transfer regarding formal professional development experiences. They attend a workshop and return to school with no stated obligation to use or even share the information. There is no real accountability for applying the learning.

To set explicit expectations and facilitate transfer in educational settings, teachers may use verbal prompts for adult learners.

■ □ ■ □ ■

To set explicit expectations and facilitate transfer in educational settings, teachers may use verbal prompts for adult learners:

"You will leave here today with a number of practical ideas that you will be able to use immediately. Keep your eyes open for ideas that will work for you."

"Keep asking the question, 'How might I use this in my classroom?' Share your ideas with others to see what they think."

"This training is just the tip of the iceberg. Picture it! What's above the surface is what we will do today. What's below the surface is a huge body of work that represents the future applications you will discover as you work with these ideas over the next few weeks, months, or years."

"You have my word. I guarantee that you will leave with ideas you can use. If you are having a challenge seeing the connection to your kids or your content, please give me a signal and we'll work through some ideas together."

"Every time you hear that little voice inside your head saying, 'Yeah, but ...,' change it to 'What if ...' and see the possibilities.

It has been well documented that explicit goal setting fosters the realization of the goals. "Write them down. Make them real." In the classroom or in professional development experiences, setting expectations for transfer is a powerful tool for setting goals and realizing them.

■□■□■

Modeling With Authentic Artifacts

Demonstrating quality performances and products is sound teaching.

Use models or artifacts to clarify what the final product might be. Demonstrating quality performances and products is sound teaching. It raises the bar and sets high expectations in the workshop setting (Joyce & Showers, 1995; Moye-Gregory, 1997).

Model examples of how the skill or strategy has been used by showing or referring to explicit classroom models. Share specific examples through real "artifacts" collected from teachers who are using the ideas across various content. Don't be afraid to do a quick "Show and Tell" to spark ideas for relevant transfer. Seeing how others have applied the ideas helps teachers see ways that they can use it in their classrooms.

Elicit examples of when the information, skill, or concept is used in other content or life situations. Ask learners to explicitly transfer this new learning, to talk about how it connects to past experiences they have had, and how it might be useful in other situations. Push learners to start an application by targeting an idea specifically. The more specific the transfer conversation is, the more likely that transfer will actually occur.

Reflecting Metacognitively

Emphasize that the levels are not meant to be judgmental.

Reflect on transfer levels by getting learners to think metacognitively about their transfer. Make them aware of the six levels of transfer (Fogarty, 1989) and have them reflect on where they are in a particular learning situation. Emphasize that the levels are not meant to be judgmental but are offered as tools for reflective conversations about how one embraces ideas for relevant transfer. This strategy works well for adult learners. A teacher working with a peer or alone may reflect by asking self-monitoring prompts, such as:

"Am I..."

Overlooking?...Missing appropriate opportunities, ignoring, persisting in former ways?

Duplicating?...Performing the drill exactly as practiced, using it with no changes, copying?

Replicating?...Tailoring to my content; customizing, applying in similar situations?

Integrating?...Combining with other ideas and situations, using with a raised consciousness and a new awareness?

Propagating?...Carrying the strategy or idea to other content; bridging, associating, mapping?

Innovating?...Inventing, taking ideas beyond the initial concept; risking diverging?

Just being aware of the different levels of transfer that can occur and recognizing which level is applicable in a particular learning situation facilitates transfer and empowers adult learners. Then, as they encounter the various levels, learners become aware of and have a way to talk about their transfer.

■□■□■

Plotting an Application

Plot an application. Have teachers record application ideas for their content and their kids. This strategy builds teachers' sense of efficacy as teachers who can make a difference (Moye-Gregory, 1997). Have learners of all ages work collaboratively, if possible, to brainstorm fruitful ideas. Use a little folder paper book—a Tiny Transfer Book— (Pete & Fogarty, 2003) to focus on the importance of transfer. Let the adult learners leave the learning with a list of ideas to try. Better yet, let them leave with a partial application already in the works. With these in hand, they can't wait to get back to the school and try some things.

> **Have learners of all ages work collaboratively, if possible, to brainstorm fruitful ideas.**

Trying Something Immediately

Try the new idea right away (Joyce & Showers, 1995; Sparks & Hirsh, 1997). It fosters transfer in teachers when they apply their learning as soon as possible. Teachers attending professional development seminars can take a new idea to the work setting as soon as possible. In fact, the sooner teachers use a new idea, the better the chances are that it will become part of their teaching repertoire. That's why it is helps foster transfer when teachers discuss possible transfer ideas in the training setting before they leave. Even better, get teachers from the training to commit to a colleague or a peer partner that they will try something the next day. Again, having learners focus on an application idea as part of the lesson may be all they

> **In fact, the sooner teachers use a new idea, the better the chances are that it will become part of their teaching repertoire.**

■ □ ■ □ ■

need to see how it works in a real context. When teachers leave the training with a "ready-to-wear" kind of application, they are eager to see how it works in their classroom.

Dialoging with Lead-ins

Use the hugging and bridging lead-ins (Fogarty, 2002; Perkins & Salomon, 1988) to connect ideas from the training setting to the classroom setting. These prompts (Marzano, Pickering, & Pollock, 2001) engage adult learners in the process of complex transfer. They create mindful connections as they lead teachers to *think back* to times they might have used and idea (if they had known about it earlier) and to *think ahead* to some possible applications in the future.

> **Connect ideas from the training setting to the classroom setting.**

Bridging lead-ins might look like these:

Overlooking: Think of an instance when the skill or strategy would be *inappropriate*. It hugs the learning but is not a proper use of it.

"I would not use _____ when ___."

"I will never ____because___."

"I probably would choose not to use____."

"One time, I overlooked the idea of___."

■ □ ■ □ ■

Duplicating: Think of a recent opportunity when you could have used the skill or strategy because it hugs the learning.

"I wish I'd known about __when___because I could've __."

"I'll steal this idea for____."

"I'd like a copy of ____."

I'm gonna borrow that idea when ___."

Replicating: Think of an adjustment to the new idea that hugs the learning, yet makes it more relevant to your content or students.

"Next time I'm gonna ____."

"By changing ____I can____."

"When I ____I'll use this to____."

"To use this , I need to____."

Integrating: Think of an analogy for the skill or strategy that clarifies the idea.

"___is like _____because both_____."

"I could combine this with____."

"An old idea this brings to mind is___."

"This seems to fit with____."

■□■□■

Propagating: Think of an opportunity for upcoming classes to use the new idea.

"In ___, I'm gonna use __to help____."

"I plan to use this___."

"I can map this strategy to____."

I can apply this idea in several ways..."

Innovating: Think of an application for a real-life setting.

"Outside of school, I could use ____when _____."

"An idea that is percolating is____."

"I see a million ways to use this..."

In my mind, I've already totally designed...."

Transfer In Reflection: Five Scenarios

In this chapter, transfer is revealed in five examples from actual classrooms. Each scenario presents a real-life example of transfer in action and, together, they provide concrete illustrations of the six levels of transfer and how they are evidenced in the classroom.

In the discussions of teacher behaviors—Overlooked Transfer, Simple Transfer, and Complex Transfer—the behaviors of the five teachers in the scenarios are used to illustrate various levels of transfer as the teachers go about using ideas from the professional development setting in their classrooms. The goal of these discussions is to foster deeper understanding of the "birds of transfer" as a tool for an individual's self-reflection on teaching or through peer partner dialogues about teaching. The reflections following scenarios are presented to give examples of how to critique transfer from the workshop to the classroom. Teachers often do their transfer process through a reflective dialogue. Yet, self-monitoring and self-assessment of transfer levels eventually become part and parcel of reflective practice.

The teachers in the scenarios are given metaphorical names that suggest their respective teaching styles (Figure 3.1). The metaphors guide the description of each teacher in the classroom.

Scenarios by Transfer Level

Overlooked Opportunity

Scenario 1: The French Teacher (The Guide)

Simple Transfer

Scenario 2: The Trigonometry Teacher (The Wizard)

Scenario 3: The Music Teacher (The Coach)

Complex Transfer

Scenario 4: The Biology Teacher (The Weaver)

Scenario 5: The Family Living Teacher (The
Counselor)

Figure 3.1

Overlooked Transfer

Teachers participating in the training did not utilize the newly introduced ideas.

Overlooked transfer is defined as an appropriate but missed instructional instance for transfer. The strategies or skills were the focus of the workshop, but the teachers participating in the training did not utilize the newly introduced ideas. Please note that overlooking of an opportunity may be intentional or unintentional by the teachers.

As readers read The French Teacher for a glimpse inside the French I class, they notice the teaching strategies and skills of the teacher as they become

■□■□■

immersed in the scene. As they continue reading to examine the reflective discussion about the actual transfer exhibited by the teacher in the scenario, readers become privy to a brief critique about how she transfers strategies from the staff room to the classroom.

The French Teacher (The Guide)

As one enters through the doors of the French class, it's as if one just stepped onto a touring bus along the streets of gay "Paree!" The excitement of the adventure that's about to begin is signaled in the animated voice of the petite, energetic tour guide.

Vacillating, staccato-style, between French and English, the Guide greets the various student passengers with personal remarks and grand, sweeping motions to accompany her facial expressions and excited tone of voice:

"Bonjour"	*"Oui"*
"Yea! Yea!"	*"N'est ce pas?"*
"Merci"	*"Parlez-vous, Francais?"*
"Mon amie"	

Amidst this settling-in process, fellow passengers cluster together and exchange greetings and remarks. Gingerly, yet briskly, *la guide d'tour* makes her way about the "bus." Varied points of interest are previewed for the group; some are traditional, historical or relevant "musts," while others are deliciously cultural and festive in nature:

■□■□■

"Today, we must review the book for the test on verbs and verb tenses."

"Did you see the piece on Jean Paul Sartre?"

"We'll be ordering "croissants;" chocolate or plain; one each; Mmmm."

"Notice the photo of the Mardi Gras."

As the formal "tour" begins, the vibrant narration of the Guide seems to gain both in volume and momentum in expectancy of what's ahead. Yet, as the bus proceeds and makes its first stop, her voice seems to settle into a more rehearsed, more reserved style, with occasional bursts of enthusiasm as an idea strikes her:

"*N'est ce pas?* Isn't that so? Isn't that right? Doesn't she? Isn't it?"

"*Mon* – masculine!"

"Let's zip through endings."

Some points on the tour seem only to be endured for their traditional value. The genuine excitement is missing from this formerly lively voice as she quiets down and instructs the passengers to read in the guide book: "Review separately; by yourself; independently."

After some time has elapsed, she looks up from her official seat, "*Fini?*" she asks, and proceeds to review the book answers with the whole group. This guidebook encapsulates the basic information that the passengers need. She knows this, and thus, uses the book to cover the basics. But to sense the real France, to bring France alive for her passengers, the Guide transmits the "essence"

■ □ ■ □ ■

of it through the cultural, festive elements so familiar to her from her own extensive experience in France.

Pantomime and acting come naturally to this teacher, as she tries to communicate this essence to these inexperienced visitors to France:

"Lunettes, glasses, little moon, (as she circles her eyes with her fingers in exaggerated gestures) and makes an aside, "lunatic; looks at the moon."

"*la neige,*" (drawing a snowman on the board and pretending to shiver uncontrollably).

"*fait du vent,*" (and whistles like the wind).

Skills of thinking are interjected to help the passengers grasp the numerous things glimpsed through the window as the bus streaks by:

"Encore. Visualize. Close your eyes. See it. Type it in."

"Look for terms and relationships."

"*Je n'est ce pas?*" You don't know. Try to describe.

The Guide's immersion in France, her love for the real France, and the memories she holds surface through her talk. Yet, the flow is abbreviated and stopped, over and over again, much like the intermittent motion of the starts and stops of the tour bus itself. The undercurrent of excitement, evident in the voice, is the one continuous thread tying together the journey.

As the metaphorical bus begins its last leg, she keeps the audience tuned in through a variety of games and activities that vary the pace and tempo of the ride as they

■ □ ■ □ ■

practice some skills in some very authentic and engaging ways:

"Bingo – Team; Team 2, call out a number; go for a square; you can coach each other."

"Memory Game; you must act out all previous words and add your word to the progressive memory game." (words: angry, search, shrug...)

"Now, chant these four times: e, es, e; Encore: Visualize; see it; type it in your brain:

     - e   - es   - e   - ous   - ez   - ent

"Find your partner. Do Ex. 1 and 2. *En Francais.* Ensemble. Review; finish the book for the test."

"Review for the culture test. Team 1, Team 2. Get close together."

"Interview your partner in French. Ask three questions. The rest of the class will guess who you interviewed. *En Francais!*"

Hoping to get students to internalize, to question, to become involved in a personal way, the Guide leads students into some reflective processing:

"Does everyone have this? Don't be shy. Scream! Yell!"

"There'll be lots of details on the test tomorrow. Go slowly."

"Look at the list. Choose carefully."

"We need your brain power."

■ □ ■ □ ■

"Reflect on the questions. Write a few words."

Winding down and nearing the end of the tour, students begin to shuffle their belongings and prepare for the exodus off the bus. France, in a flash, then onto the next tour.

Discussion of Overlooked Transfer

An overlooked opportunity for transfer occurred during the opening minutes of a class in The French Teacher scenario. During training, the Guide elaborated, demonstrated, and practiced the skill of prediction. The trainer suggested that teachers have students predict what would happen next as part of the introductory material to their lessons. However, in her classroom, the Guide welcomed the students entering the classroom and proceeded to delineate the day's work rather than asking students to connect their work from the day before to what the day's agenda might include.

Another example of overlooked opportunity occurred in The French Teacher scenario. During the training that the Guide attended, the instructor stressed the theory involving extended use of student-to-student interactions to provide frequent opportunities for student articulation. Strategies were then introduced, modeled, and practiced with application examples for pre-learning during the learning and post-learning activities. But, when helping students review material for a test, the Guide overlooked the opportunity to use these interactive and cooperative strategies and instructed students to use the text to review by themselves.

■□■□■

In another instance, the concept of awareness and control over one's own thinking was emphasized as a major thread throughout the training. This metacognitive behavior requires students to plan, monitor, and evaluate their decisions. In one classroom episode in The French Teacher, although the Guide asked students to make individual choices, she overlooked the opportunity to let them justify their decisions.

Based on situations similar to the ones just described, overlooked opportunity for transfer is an easily recognized category of transfer.

Simple Transfer

Simple transfer is defined as the observed application of a skill or strategy in a classroom situation that is very similar to the training example in both content and context. The transfer is almost automatic and sometimes a direct copy. At other times, the transfer is adjusted slightly. But in both situations, the transfer is fairly simple. With that idea of simple transfer in mind, readers will find examples of how teachers transfer some things from the workshop to the classroom in The Trigonometry Teacher and The Music Teacher scenarios. Discussion critiques instances from the two classrooms following each scenario.

The transfer is almost automatic and sometimes a direct copy. At other times, the transfer is adjusted slightly.

The Trigonometry Teacher (The Wizard)

Bounding about the room as if he had springs on his shoes, the Wizard teases his student

■ □ ■ □ ■

audience/participants with puzzles, riddles, and reasoning.

"Chris, give it a shot. [Chris chooses Door Number 4.] Now tell us the answer you've selected and why."

"Process of elimination? Good technique. Fantastic. Why?"

"Another one. [He chooses Door Number 3.] Ratio. Why?"

"Great. We did just finish talking about (ratio) the day before. Talking about what we did the day before helps us get to today."

"Hangman. Solve puzzle."

C O M P L E M E N T A R Y

The Wizard lets students know that they are part of the show. He tells them that he teaches them, they teach each other, and they teach themselves. He also provides a constant patter of feedback and reinforcement that, though given in a playful manner, seems to honor and dignify every answer:

"This group is hot."

"Hear some good talking, here."

"Holy Smokes! You got this? How?"

"No idea? Remember you can go to other groups."

"Is this all? Check with others. Talk to teammates."

"I'll tell you. That's the right one. Now, you tell me why."

■ □ ■ □ ■

"Bingo, Linda's ready."

The audience knows the Wizard is the "wise one"; yet his use of "magic" as he searches among them for evidence of thinking intrigues them. He challenges them in such an entertaining manner that they are almost tricked into postures of wonderment as he captures their interest and catches them thinking:

"What is the geometric mean?"

"Oh, listen I feel a theorem coming on," as a student carefully states her idea.

"Ever play the pyramid game? What do these— sewer pipe, mountain, ski hill—have in common? Give one word."

"Slope! Silly. You've already figured out that this is leading to something."

The Wizard knows his students well and uses clever humor throughout his class that signals he is right on target with what's going on:

"He has it in his head. That's why he's not writing it down."

"I thought I had to dust the cobwebs – but I need a snow shovel."

"David, this is the easiest one (question) in America."

"He doesn't believe it. Convince him."

"I can help you with it, but I can't re-teach the whole course."

■ □ ■ □ ■

"I thought about inventing graph paper Kleenex.
Why is that a good idea?"

The Wizard signals expectations that will transfer
learning beyond the classroom and into future academic
or life situations:

"If you're going to be successful quizzer – when
you hit the door – you must 'Learn it for life,
not just for the test'."

This wizardry continues throughout the session as the
Wizard entices students into entertainingly complex
problem-solving situations. His pacing is fast as he poses
question after question. Expectations are there for students
to respond and justify:

"Door Number 4 Linear Equation? Want to
change your idea?"

"What do you think?"

"Why only consider positive values?"

"Have you seen this one before? Yep, it was on
the test. How many wrote 4, not -4?"

The Wizard relishes his games and exhibits a
contagious energy and enthusiasm for his art. He believes
that kids are used to being entertained and puts that
knowledge to work for him in the classroom:

"Now you might like this one."

"Why is *Jeopardy* the best game show? Yes –
they give the answer, you ask the question."

■ □ ■ □ ■

"In the relay race, there will be five rounds. And
remember goose egg gets double points.
That keeps us all in the race."

His energetic quizzing forces students to hypothesize,
analyze, verify, and evaluate:

Forced Hypothesis Question: "What was the
name of the last chapter? How does it
connect?"

Forced Analysis Question: "What makes #4
different?"

Forced Verification Question: "Algebra I: Algebra
II: Trig. Right, Jeff. Why is trig like
geometry? How did you get it?"

Forced Evaluation Question: "Did we accomplish
it?"

The Wizard's lightning speed and unpredictable
targeting keeps students alert and involved. Yet, support
is always evident and feedback is specific and pointed:

"Anyone need help?"

"Tests – very fine. 23/30 average."

He varies the interactions depending on the purpose:

"We'll need partners for this one."

"Girls take odd rows. Boys take even."

"Teams by rows."

Above all, as the Wizard works his spell on the captive
audience, he spins a constant tale of why they are doing

■ □ ■ □ ■

what they are doing. His modeling of explanations and reasons overrides every aspect of the interaction. The students leave with an understanding not only of what and how but also with a sense of why:

> "Why do I make you memorize theorems and definitions? Because in mathematics, the system is built from scratch. If pieces are missing, the pyramid tumbles. You must memorize certain things."

> "Don't let your algebra get in the way of trigonometry."

> "What are some memory tricks? Learn part now; before school ends, learn another section; before tomorrow, learn rest; or tape record and play in your sleep."

> "Bring a calculator. I will make sure you know how to use it."

The Wizard sums up his feelings when he says, "I don't come to work. I come to school. I have fun, too."

Discussion of Simple Transfer: The Wizard

One example of simple transfer is cited in the Wizard's classroom. Requiring students to listen to each other's answer and respond to each other as well as to the teacher was a student-to-student strategy stressed in a training that the Wizard in The Trigonometry Teacher attended. The Wizard transmitted teacher expectations for this student-to-student interaction by responding to an incomplete student response by suggesting that another student was responsible to pick up where the first student had stopped. This behavior just repeated the behavior that occurred during training and presents a good example of simple transfer, along the lines of a Dan, the Duplicator.

In addition, the Wizard evidenced simple transfer in another situation. The training specified a model of making connections between prior knowledge and new learning through deliberate strategies that required student reflective processing. The Wizard replicated when he used a method very similar to one that was used in the training when he asked students to recall if they had seen a similar problem before.

The Music Teacher (The Coach)

The climate is informal, with student performers funneling into the tiered choral room. Activity swirls around the grand piano placed strategically in the center of the semicircular tiers.

Students handle the management of materials and equipment with efficient routine procedures, which were learned at some time earlier in the year. Various students systematically manage attendance, announcements, money collections (for the full agenda of extracurricular events), and books and sheet music. They appear responsibly in charge and seem to tend to the tasks with pride and care:

"Management."

"Fruit?" (student handles)

"Symphony tickets, up front." (Another student collects money.)

"Bus, after 1:00 p.m."

■ □ ■ □ ■

Student: "I have an announcement."

A steady stream of students stop by the piano area, making requests, excuses, or just to remark in passing as they move to designated spots on the rows of tiered risers. The teacher reacts personally to each, fielding the multitude of needed decisions in a friendly, sometimes non-verbal, expedient manner.

The warmest of smiles lights her face and her total demeanor suggests enthusiasm for this role that requires much of her time and energy, both in and out of the school setting.

All this commotion is abruptly halted as her coaching posture is assumed and a chord is sounded on the piano to signal attention and readiness for the work at hand.

"Warm-ups, first."

"Jeff, turn around."

"Care!"

"Sit tall."

"Quiet."

"Breathe."

"Jeffrey?"

(The Coach models the expected behavior, smiling as she waits expectantly for their full focus.)

The energy level is incredible. Pacing is brisk, the content heavy. A sense of purpose pervades the

■ □ ■ □ ■

atmosphere for live performance dates are many. Just as in any performing art, the "show" is the goal.

Preparations for upcoming events keep interest piqued and the pressure on:

"Madrigals. Methodist Church." (In an aside to the unknowing visitor, the Coach says, "We've been selected as one of six groups to go to Allerton in March.")

"Sunrise service."

"Madrigals – concert in hall before band and orchestra practice."

Throughout the rehearsal, this music coach takes the lead in accompanying each piece both vocally and technically. With fingers flying across the keys, she grandly mouths the lyrics, sets the tempo, plays the melody, and interjects cues to signal direction, style, and intent of the music:

"Let's run this section."

"Stay with me."

"Watch the pitch."

"Yes. Better!"

"Do we look motivated?"

All in the room are immersed in this world of music and performing. Yet, time is allotted for special interests of students, aside from the traditional high school repertoire, as individual interests and talents are showcased:

"Extra credit performances. Who's first?"

"West Side Story."

■ □ ■ □ ■

"Next? Beth."

"Friends, by M. W. Smith."

Yet, as these young people perform, they instinctively rely on the inherent talents of the Coach. Their appreciation (and awe) of her talents is seen in the requests for accompaniment. Regardless of the selection, they expect her to know it ... and she rarely disappoints them in their expectations of the expert:

"West Side Story. Will you play for me?"

"Play with me? I'm having trouble with the rhythm."

"One voice lesson. Will you run through with me?"

Expectations are high. The school has a reputation to uphold and the students are aware of this. They are motivated to excel:

"Sectionals. Last chance to fix-up. One week from Thursday."

"You have one minute to review text. Then, we'll do from memory."

"OK, you know what you have to do."

The experienced Coach models the behaviors of direct instruction of a skill. Directions are clear, concise, and crisp. As students strive for perfection in their performance, Coach monitors activities constantly as she laces practice with pointed feedback that is both positive and critical:

"Class. We'll take the alto section."

"Sopranos, do you see where you are?"

"Good. Chopped."

"I need a tenor."

"We're starting."

"Bravo."

"Tenors. Sing with them. Then cut out and let them do the refrain."

"Phrase ending. Not too fast."

To clarify her directions, this teacher relies on vivid analogies to make her instructions concrete and explicit. These mental pictures are often accompanied with the gestures and pantomime:

"Swell, like an organ opening the pedal."

"Tune it, ... hold on...like an oxygen tank on your back."

"Shh – spit it out like pulling taffy. Look!" (as she demonstrates).

"...swimming a little bit in that section."

"...like an orange peel inside out in the back of your throat."

Throughout the intense, fast-paced classes, Coach interacts intensely with the whole group, while also intervening with specific cues and feedback for the different sections and for individual performers:

"Listen! Listen! Balance the chord; space back here, in tune."

"Shape it, Carol!"

■□■□■

"Altos! Flat!"

"Space it back. Drop out altos."

As students see the Coach model images through pantomime, by stressing posture, and by using facial expression, tongue position, and the set of the jaw, they mirror the skillful performance of the experienced coach. Reflective imaging in this vocal music class epitomizes the same metaphorical mirroring behavior used in the coaching of athletic champions:

"Sit tall." (She models.)

"Shape your mouth. Pucker! Pucker!" (She exaggerates a pucker and deadpans, as students dissolve in laughter.)

"Lips barely touching..." (showing them).

"Sit tall. Breathe!" (as she demonstrates the breathing).

Aware of the need to move and restructure to keep the intensity and focus, Coach often rearranges the class or gives instructions to change stance at their places:

"Quickly. Form a big circle."

"Five around the piano."

"Stand in a circle. Mix up."

"All cluster around the piano for this part."

"Stand in formation."

Metacognition is built into this instructor's repertoire. Instinctively understanding the value for monitoring and

■ □ ■ □ ■

evaluating one's own behavior, Coach models an on-going talk-aloud strategy that students tend to internalize over time. Her ear for mistakes is uncanny as she targets problem spots in the group, adjusts immediately, and carries the group through the piece:

> "What's happening to pitch?"

> "Last two measures. Right. See the connection."

> "Whatever happens, stay with me."

> "That's better, sopranos; better vowel on a."

> "…takes too much concentration. Sections are mixed up."

> "Keep tapping quarter notes."

Evaluation is requested as well as given, as Coach guides her players toward improvement, synchronization, and pride in doing their best:

> "What will make this phrase better?"

> "What about vowels?"

> "Altos. What are you doing? Look at the notes."

"Compare this to the performance last night." (Student answer: "More balanced" – with his explanation of what he meant.)

Discussion of Simple Transfer: the Coach

As an instance of simple transfer, the Coach in the Music Teacher attended a training in which the strategy of modeling was stressed as a key element in teaching skills explicitly to students. The Coach used this strategy while demonstrating the mouth position for a particular sound. This concrete modeling was very similar to physical examples used during the training days—an example of Laura the Look-Alike Penguin who replicates.

Complex Transfer

Complex transfer is defined as an observed application that is enhanced, abstracted, or greatly modified from the content and/or context of the original training or instruction. Complex transfer is mindful. It often takes explicit connection-making or thoughtful integration to create sophisticated applications. As readers dive into the last two teacher scenarios, they will see a Biology teacher and a Family Living teacher at work in their respective classrooms.

The Biology Teacher (The Weaver)

With patience and precision, the Weaver intertwines the threads of his discipline into an intricate pattern of exquisite design as he instructs his student apprentices. The pattern begins with a skillful approach to questioning students as he asks, probes, and extends:

"Why?"

"Explain?"

"Then?...Then?...Then?..."

Complex transfer is mindful.

"What else?"

"Who agrees? Disagrees? Why?"

The artistry of the questioning pattern is elaborated as Weaver intentionally introduces each point by weaving the name of the student and the student's response into a spiraling question and response design:

"Dave says..."

"Katie might be on to something..."

"Ken shakes his head..."

"Tatiana thinks..."

"Let's build on Scott's comment..."

"Victor, right on the money..."

His enthusiasm for his craft is shared with students as he delights in the wonders of science:

"Isn't it amazing that every single inherited characteristic is determined by five elements?"

"Imagine, red hair, blue eyes, each dictated into every single cell."

"We're talking plants, right? So how does the water get all the way to the top of a redwood tree?"

"Let's solve the mystery. Why are some groups seeing change in the water color and others are not?"

Weaver's expectations for student thinking and for cooperative interactions are signaled both verbally and non-verbally with humor and warmth as he weaves his way throughout the openings in the rows of desks:

> "Scott, draw some parameters on this."

> "Victor, what about..."

> "Steve needs help. Who's gonna bail him out?"

> "Tim, are you catching some dreams?"

The complexity of his weaving technique is further illustrated as Weaver masterfully integrates lecture information and textbook references into an already complex verbal interchange. He gingerly laces the lecture with questions that lead students to hypothesize, predict, evaluate, compare, and conclude:

> "Replication, rather than duplication – half new
>   molecules, half old. Do you buy that?"

> "Isotope, another form of an element."

> "Notice the question in Watson and ... (text)?"

> "There are a lot of appendices. Turn to the back of
>   your book..."

But the design of the weave begins to reveal more layers of intricate, deliberate patterns. Weaver delicately manipulates the cloth of this classroom as he introduces the threads of higher level thinking:

> "Looking at the data, what conclusions can you
>   draw?"

> "What evidence supports your statement?"

> "I suggest you compare RNA and DNA."

■□■□■

"Let's hypothesize...one more possible theory..."

"Predict what you think will happen."

"Can we capture the key concept?"

"Generalize what we've said..."

As the students are drawn into this beautifully designed web of intrigue, Weaver illustrates the conceptual information with colorful and relevant analogies. By describing these concrete examples that are familiar to students, he anchors the new learning throughout the patterned interaction with these carefully selected mental images:

"...pairing replication, like a zipper with teeth on one side."

"How many have worked a jigsaw? Anyone start on the outside, the boundary? Why?"

"Just like at the Indy 500. Drivers don't just turn a key. A guy stands behind the car and ignites the turbo charger."

"It's similar to a squeeze coin purse ..."

"You've seen the paratroopers come out the door like a chain reaction ..."

"Like a slinky, stretched out ..."

Using his skill as the master weaver, Weaver integrates the patterns of interpersonal interaction into an encompassing design. Taking advantage of the laboratory in the back of the room, he frequently organizes small groups of students around the tables that have been carefully equipped and set up with the necessary materials:

> "Use the dice rolls to determine the number..."

> "Illustrate the final creature you've created showing all the critical attributes."

> "With your lab partners, make a classification key for another group's creature."

> "Determine in your groups the roles for each member."

> "Kids who finish first, act as consultants to other groups."

Paralleling the interpersonal interactions of cooperative groups, Weaver also incorporates interactions with the concepts and materials. Both pencil/paper advance organizers and hands-on laboratory experiments are introduced into instructional strategies:

> "Using the morphological grid, or matrix ..."

> "Before the session begins, mingle (using question sheet) and see how many can answer any of three questions (list questions)."

Adding the final touches to his intricate pattern of classroom interactions, Weaver knits the metacognitive element into the finished fabric of his teaching. His structured processing and discussions help students stand back from and look at the lesson at hand as a strategy or skill for further use. This is the thread he uses to tie the learning together. Through this metacognitive element, he

■ ⌐ ■ □ ■

helps students extrapolate the essence of an idea and apply the concepts across curricular disciplines and into life situations:

> "Did anyone find out from the math teacher about the double helix we were talking about in here (science)?"

> "You should be writing notes in your thinking log throughout – about the theory of evolution."

> "A practical application; the pipes in your home all have calcium deposits... more pressure... dribble..."

The Weaver further illustrates his mastery and understanding of the learning process with a subtle but powerful metacognitive strategy at the end of the session:

"Take the last five minutes to get organized for your next class." Not surprisingly, he continues to weave the threads of his own learning into various applications in his life outside the biology lab.

> "I'm going to use the web strategy with my real estate class tomorrow night."

> "I can't wait to teach the gifted summer school (3rd graders) so I can try these ideas out there."

> "I presented at the Illinois Science Teachers Association and I used the create-a-creature classification lesson."

> "I'll be presenting again in Chicago in November. I'm gonna use the people search, again."

■□■□■

Discussion of Complex Transfer: The Weaver

To begin a reflective discussion of complex transfer, the Weaver in The Biology Teacher scenario exhibited behavior that showed complex transfer in a particular interaction that required students not only to listen to each other and respond but also to engage in a constructive controversy. In the scenario, the Weaver acknowledged that the first student did not believe it and instructed another student to convince the first student. This exemplifies a complex application of the student-to-student response strategy because the Weaver had enhanced the simpler response pattern practiced in the training by extracting and calling for the justification element of reflective processing. This represents a level of integrated transfer, as depicted by the Jonathan Livingston Seagull metaphor. The teacher is integrating a skillful response strategy as he is more aware of how response strategies work.

In another example, explicit thinking skills stressing the need to discuss the menu of operations needed to execute the skill were modeled in a training that the Weaver attended. The Weaver exhibited complex transfer of the training model by using the concept with the compare-and-contrast thinking skill, which had not been specifically taught in the training. In addition to transferring to a new skill (by asking students to compare and contrast the concepts of duplication and replication), he delineated a menu of operations (by instructing students to find both similarities and differences as they completed the task), which further enhanced the transfer of the training examples. This is an example of Samantha, the Soaring Eagle at work, because the transfer was clever, unique, and skillfully relevant.

Throughout a training attended by the Weaver, the use of a learning log for both teachers and students was emphasized. The Weaver applied the concept of the log in an original way. He instructed students to keep a log throughout the semester to record their thoughts on the theory of evolution. Although the log entry ideas in the training had focused on recording thoughts about one specific learning instance, the Weaver enhanced the modeled logging technique with the addition of entries made over a period of time for one topic treated in the class. His level of transfer reached the level of Samantha, the Soaring Eagle, because he introduced several enhancements—the year-long journal and the themed journal.

The Family Living Teacher (The Counselor)

The focus is on fashion, food, and family as students in the Home Economics sections learn to "Celebrate Life." The settings vary with activities planned for typical classrooms, the day care center, kitchen units, sewing rooms, and video recording studios. The diversity of programs depicts the diversity of life itself, as this caring teacher assumes the role of counselor and sets the climate for learning:

"Let's get together in a circle."

"We've changed the desks from rows to circles
    so we can see and her each other."

"Let's go around the circle."

As she quietly monitors the discussion, Counselor questions from a guiding or psychological perspective, dignifying every answer and focusing on individual worth:

> "So you're saying... (paraphrases)."

> "I've gotten a new insight." (honors)

> "What would a compromise approach be?"

> "Yes. That seems basic to good mental health, doesn't it?"

> "What did you discover?"

> "What else?"

> "Dave, how do you feel?"

Always presenting a warm, yet dignified manner, Counselor smiles and reflects on the student response, then pushes the class toward analysis, synthesis, and evaluation:

> "What are you hearing? Can you summarize?"

> "As you review, find the questions you think you know the answers to. Then ask those questions to others to verify."

> "Prepare selected readings. Be ready to compare."

> "Watch a friend's presentation (of a children's book) and give feedback for improvement."

The diversity of skills necessary for the many areas of learning is evidenced in the topics listed on the Spring program, "Celebrate Life":

"Nutritional Notes" (Analyzing the elements of healthy and nutritious meals.)

"Color Highlights" (Comparing and contrasting color tones for cosmetics and fashion.)

"Child life and Literature" (Dramatizing the essence of the storyline and analyzing the lessons in the story.)

"Child Development Studies" (Analyzing the developmental stages and inferring the implications for parents and teachers.)

"Stress" (Evaluating and Problem-Solving.)

"We Manage" (Sequencing, prioritizing, organizing and researching.)

"Fashion Display" (Designing, critiquing.)

"Commercial Foods" (Decision-making.)

Projects with concrete products provide the perfect setting for the integrated series of skills involved in the creative process. Students generate ideas, put their ideas together in a novel way, attend to details by analyzing problem areas, revise, enhance, critique, and, finally, celebrate a job well done through various productions targeted to selective audiences:

"Prepare a piece of children's literature. Use puppets, costumes, scenery, props, voice changes...whatever you think."

"We'll videotape each presentation so you can see yourself."

■ □ ■ □ ■

"The spring program "Celebrate Life" was a huge
success. We have to move to a larger hall."

"The spring program may be the only opportunity
some of these kids have to be on stage...and
they are great. They do a beautiful job."

Counselor takes full advantage of the practical arts
format that provides the ideal setting for structuring informal
small groups and face-to-face interactions. She is particularly
sensitive to the benefits of such structure.

By tailoring each interaction for optimal emotional
support, Counselor prepares carefully for the lesson.
Sometimes, large circles are deemed best for personal
sharing:

"Let's use the large circle so we can hear each
other."

"The role-playing characters should sit in the center
of the semi-circle so we can view your faces as
you talk."

Other times, the interaction pattern preferred is small teams:

"For the parent rights scenarios, find two other 'law
partners' and form a law firm."

"Build cases for the parents with the law in mind.
Each partner in your firm should help support
your stand."

"For the dress rehearsals, find a partner who will
watch and tell you what it looks like."

"Work in teams for the show. Prepare together."

"I'll meet the teams in the video room."

■ □ ■ □ ■

The counseling perspective seems at the root of every exchange as Counselor perceives the underlying problems or circumstances surrounding the student and opts for the solution or action that dignifies and develops the person. The flexibility is noted over and over:

> "One girl had been very mouthy yesterday, and the kids sensed it and handled it."

> "We'll finish the video that _____ brought to share."

> "I planned for the parent's right law teams, but we can start those tomorrow."

> "I noticed you were really touched by the film. I almost cried, too."

> "I had planned a different lesson, but the slide production "Shades" deals with peer pressure and seems so pertinent. We'll catch up this week."

Although, at times, the students think they've maneuvered her, Counselor is fully aware of what's going on. Her authorship of several texts in the field, *Relationships: A Study in Human Behavior* and *Children: A Study in Individual Behavior*, provides evidence that she is tuned acutely to student behavior. In turn, she leads them toward self-awareness or she provides opportunities for self-processing:

> "Can we make this work?"

> "I think it's important to watch your own videotape so you can see yourself and think about things before you present to the kids."

■□■□■

"Ask yourself if you know it? Then ask yourself if
    you know it well enough to write about it."

"Isn't it interesting how the weather affects a
    group?"

"Why do you think we all like the weekends so
    much?"

"Do an attitude analysis. See how you feel?"

When conflicts arise between cognitive instruction and
human needs, Counselor understands that the affective
domain rules the cognitive. She opens herself up to peer
criticism, perhaps, but one senses a sureness within her that
she lives the values she believes as she provides a richness
of opportunities for her students.

"A teacher asked me how I could let those kids perform
on stage when they were such amateurs. But I believe they
need that experience."

Discussion of Complex Transfer: The Counselor

Enhancing the cooperative learning model with a novel
approach, the Counselor in The Family Living Teacher
scenario formed groups of "law partners" to examine cases
on parents' rights. She further structured the goal of
interdependence by suggesting that students first gather their
information as partners and then join with other partners to
form a law firm. The law firm was then responsible to
defend the case in point. This modification to the
cooperative group model displays complex transfer because
the modeled behavior from a training attended by the

■ □ ■ □ ■

Counselor was greatly enhanced by the specific teacher-added application. This is a rich and classic case of Cathy, the Carrier Pigeon transfer. The Counselor skillfully propagated or mapped the strategy into law firm language.

Conclusion

As shown by the organization and content of this book, the transfer strategies are intended for the adult learner. The transfer concept is easily introduced in professional development situations, with assigned peer coaches working together to track and reflect on their transfer. Then, as teachers become aware of the transfer in student learning situations, they gradually introduce these ideas to students. That is when students become metacognitively aware of their own levels of transfer and application.

Appendix

Student Transfer: A Look at ...

Student Transfer: A Look at Ollie Head-in-the-Sand Ostrich

Looks Like...	Sounds Like...
This learner doesn't really get it. He does the exercises but has no real awareness of the long-term applications. He overlooks any real opportunities to use or to incorporate the practices learned. Ollie, in the classroom, doesn't take ownership in the learning situation. He simply goes through the motions. He misses the obvious opportunities for transfer.	*"I get it right on the worksheet, but I always forget how to use punctuation consistently in my writing."* *"I don't see how I'm ever going to use these formulae in real life."* *"Why are we learning all this stuff about elements in chemistry class? It has not applications in my life."*

Figure A.1

Student Transfer: A Look at Dan, the Drilling Woodpecker

Looks Like...	Sounds Like...
This learner performs the skills exactly as practiced. She duplicates the original with no thought of varying it or personalizing it. Dan, the Duplicator will repeat the process verbatim and may actually have little understanding of what she is doing. Yet, she's working on an automatic level of transfer that demonstrates some degree of application. Therefore, celebrate the application effort and eventually, coach this learner to tailor the ideas for more personal and relevant transfer.	*"Mine is not to reason why, just invert and multiply when you are dividing fractions."* *"I've always had three paragraphs in my essays-a beginning, a middle and end."* *"I use the problem-solving strategy that works for me. I always draw a picture of the problem just like we practiced."*

Figure A.2

Student Transfer: A Look at Laura, the Look-alike Penguin.

Looks Like...	Sounds Like...
This learner understands that she must make some refinements to the newly learned ideas in order to use them effectively. Laura will tailor and customize a strategy to fit their specific situation. She readily tweaks an idea. She naturally "tinkers" with ideas and designs the application differently to meet her particular needs. This learner adjusts and refines.	*"Paragraphing means I have three indents per page, but I am careful where I use them."* *"I always use a web as a pre-writing strategy."* *I have to personalize an idea to make it my own. Otherwise, it doesn't make sense to me.*

Figure A.3

Student Transfer Level: Jonathan Livingston Seagull

Looks Like...	Sounds Like...
Jonathan finds it easy to integrate new ideas into his work. This learner is aware and mindfully uses an idea by weaving it into other preexisting things he knows and does. This learner is a natural integrator who is able to blend the new with the old and get fresh results. This is the first level of complex transfer in which application is not automatic, but requires some thoughtful application.	*"Ever since we learned about making predictions when we read, I've been making prediction, at every commercial, when I watch television."* *"I use WordArt, now, whenever I use Power Point to create a presentation."* *"I've always used a lot of sources in my research paper, but now I prefer to do anecdotal citations."*

Figure A.4

■ □ ■ □ ■

Student Transfer: A Look at Cathy, the Carrier Pigeon.

Looks Like...	Sounds Like...
This learner very consciously carries an idea to a new application. This may be transfer in the same subject or even in a different class. Cathy sees connections and automatically "maps" ideas within and across content. This learner, literally, propagates the instructional landscape with many applications of the idea. This is the ideal learner because she is "scouting" for possible uses; she's very proactive as a learner.	*Parent: "Tania suggested we brainstorm our vacation ideas and then rank them. She said this works with things you do in school."* *" I use the word parameter all the time now that I know what it means."* *"I use text messaging with all my friends. It's such a fun way to communicate and it's something that our parents don't really know how to do... or to decode."*

Figure A.5

■ □ ■ □ ■

Student Transfer: A Look at Samantha, the Soaring Eagle.

Looks Like...	Sounds Like...
This learner is a risk-taker who goes above and beyond the required applications. Sam is so creative, he sees many ways to elaborate or change an idea to make it unique and "just right" for what he's trying to do. This learner is an innovator who diverges readily and often comes up with novel applications. The innovator is flexible, fluent and elaborative in his thinking and finds it natural to synthesize and put new ideas out there.	*"After studying the flow chart graphic, I decided to make a 3D flow chart. It's called a Rube Goldberg Machine."* *"Rather than write about Martin Luther King, I've made a video of a role play in which you can hear his speeches."* *"Instead of simply prioritizing my ideas, I ranked them by using a card game. That way I could keep changing my mind and rearranging them."*

Figure A.6.

Bibliography

Bellanca, J., & Fogarty, R. (2003). *Blueprints for achievement in the cooperative classroom.* Thousand Oaks, CA: Corwin.

Bradley, A. (1999). Zeroing in on teachers. *Education Week, 18*(17), 46–52.

Caine, R. N., & Caine, G. (1994). *Making connections: Teaching and the human brain.* New York: Addison-Wesley/Innovative Learning Publications.

College Begins in Kindergarten. (2000). *Trust: News.* Washington, DC: The Education Trust.

Costa, A., & Kallick, B. (2000). *Discovering and exploring habits of mind.* Alexandria, VA: Association for Supervision and Curriculum Development.

DeSchryver, D. (2003). The Doyle report. *Spotlight,* Issue 3.2.

Dewey, J. (1938). *Experience and education.* New York: Collier.

Eisner, E. W. (1979). *Educational imagination: On the design and evaluation of school programs.* New York: Macmillan.

Fogarty, R. (1989). *From training to transfer: The role of creativity in the adult learner.* Unpublished doctoral dissertation, Loyola University of Chicago, Chicago, IL.

Fogarty, R. (2001a). *Differentiated learning: Different strokes for different folks.* Chicago: Fogarty & Associates.

Fogarty, R. (2001b) *Finding the time and the money: For professional development.* Chicago: Fogarty & Associates.

Fogarty, R. (2001c). *Making sense of the research: On the brain and learning.* Chicago: Fogarty & Associates.

Fogarty, R. (2001d). *A mentoring model for our teachers: Centers of pedagogy.* Chicago: Fogarty & Associates.

Fogarty, R. (2001e). *So, You Wannabe a Consultant: Notebook and Study Guide.* Chicago: Robin Fogarty & Associates.

Fogarty, R. (2001f). *Student learning standards: A blessing in disguise.* Chicago: Fogarty & Associates.

Fogarty, R. (2001g). *Teachers make a the difference: A framework of quality.* Chicago: Fogarty & Associates.

Fogarty, R. (2002). *Brain compatible classrooms* (2nd ed.). Thousand Oaks, CA: Corwin.

Fogarty, R., & Bellanca,. J. (1991). *Patterns for thinking, patterns for transfer.* Palatine, IL: Skylight Publishing.

Fogarty, R., Perkins, D., & Barell, J. (1992). *The mindful school: How to teach for transfer.* Palatine, IL: IRI/Skylight Training and Publishing.

Haycock, K. (1998). Good teaching matters … a lot. *The Education Trust.* Summer 1998.

Haycock, K. (1999, March). Good teaching matters … a lot. *NSDC Results,* 45–46.

Haycock, K. (1998). Good teaching matters: How well-qualified teachers can close the gap. *Thinking k-16,* 3(2), 2.

Joyce, B. (1999). The great literacy problem and success for all. *Phi Delta Kappan, 81*(2), 129–131.

Joyce, B., & Showers, B. (1995). *Student cchievement through staff development.* White Plaines, NY: Longman.

Knowles, M. S. (1984). *The adult learner: A neglected species* (3rd ed.). Houston, TX: Gulf Publishing Co.

■ □ ■ □ ■

Knowles, M.S. (1980). *The modern practice of adult education: From pedagogy to andragogy* (2d ed.). New York: Cambridge Books.

Kohn, A. (1999, December 9). Tests that cheat students. *New York Times*, OP-ED, p. A31.

Marzano, R., Pickering, D., & Pollock, J. (2001). *Classroom instruction that works*. Alexandria, VA: Association for Supervision and Curriculum Development.

Moye, V. (1997). *Conditions that support transfer for change*. Arlington Heights, IL: IRI/Skylight Training and Publishing.

No Child Left Behind Act of 2001. (2001). Washington, DC: U.S. Department of Education.

O' Conner, E. (2002, October). *Transforming leadership for learning* [keynote address]. Association for Supervision and Curriculum Development, Seventh Conference on Teaching and Learning. New Orleans, LA.

Olebe, M., Jackson, A., & Danielson, C. (1999). Investing in beginning teachers—the California model. *Education Leadership, 56*(8), 41–44.

Olson, L., & Hoff, D. J. (1999). Teaching tops agenda at summit. *Education Week, 19*(6),1, 20.

Perkins, D., & Salomon, G. (1988) Teaching for transfer. *Educational Leadership, 46*(1), 22–23.

Pete, B. M., &. Fogarty, R. J. (2003a). *Nine best practices that make the difference*. Thousand Oaks, CA: Corwin.

Pete, B. M., & Fogarty, R. J. (2003b). *Twelve brain principles that make the difference*. Thousand Oaks, CA: Corwin.

Piaget, J. (1970). Piaget's theory. In P. Mussen (Ed.), *Carmichael's manual of child psychology.* New York: Wiley.

Rose, L., & Gallup, A. M. (1999). The 31st annual Phi Delta Kappa/Gallup Poll of the public's attitudes toward the public schools [Insert]. *Phi Delta Kappan, 81*(1), 41–56.

Scavone, N. (2003). *National board certification: Journey in professional development.* Chicago: Robin Fogarty & Associates.

Schalock, D., Schalock, M., & Myton, D. (1998). Effectiveness— along with quality—should be the focus [Response to At Odds: Quality Assurance for Teachers]. *Phi Delta Kappan, 79*(6), 468–470.

Schmoker, M. (1996). *Results: The key to continuous school improvement.* Alexandria, VA: Association for Supervision and Curriculum Development.

Schmoker, M. (1998). *Why results? Restructuring brief* (No. 17). Santa Rosa: California Professional Development Consortia.

Schmoker, M. (2003). Planning for failure? *Education Week, 22*(22), 39.

Sparks, D. (1999). What teachers should expect from staff development [Advertisement]. *Education Week, 18*(41), 50.

Sparks, D., & Hirsh, S. (1997). *A new vision for staff development.* Alexandria, VA: Association for Supervision and Curriculum Development.

Wise, A. E. (1999). Commentary: A hard-won system begins to pay off. *Education Week, 18*(36), 48, 68.

Wolfe, P. (2001). *Brain matters.* Alexandria, VA: Association for Supervision and Curriculum Development.

■ □ ■ □ ■

CORWIN

A SAGE Company

The Corwin logo—a raven striding across an open book—represents the union of courage and learning. Corwin is committed to improving education for all learners by publishing books and other professional development resources for those serving the field of PreK–12 education. By providing practical, hands-on materials, Corwin continues to carry out the promise of its motto: **"Helping Educators Do Their Work Better."**